# The i'Mpossible Project
# Lemonade Stand

## Volume III

### A Special Edition

## Joshua Rivedal & Kathleen Myre

### 20 Authors

Skookum Hill Publishing
Los Angeles, CALIFORNIA

2020

Copyright © 2020 by Joshua Rivedal.

All rights reserved. No part of this publication may be reproduced, distributed or transmitted in any form or by any means, including photocopying, recording, or other electronic or mechanical methods, without the prior written permission of the author. If you would like to do any of the above, please seek permission first by contacting josh@iampossibleproject.com or the address below.

Skookum Hill Publishing
369 S. Doheny Dr. #197
Beverly Hills, CA 90211

Thematic Editor: Joshua Rivedal
Cover Design: Rose Miller
Book Layout: Joshua Rivedal

Ordering Information:
Quantity sales. Special discounts are available on quantity purchases by corporations, associations, and others. For details, contact the "Special Sales Department" at the address above. Contact the author directly at http://www.iampossibleproject.com or josh@iampossibleproject.com for special fund-raising opportunities for charitable organizations.

The i'Mpossible Project: Lemonade Stand, Volume III/ Joshua Rivedal, Kathleen Myre
ISBN 978-1-7336276-5-8

# Acknowledgements

We, Kathleen and Josh, cannot express how grateful we are for the support of the folks listed below. They have all helped champion this book, while some of them have even held, loved, defended, and comforted one or more of the twenty authors in this book. To our twenty authors, we salute your bravery, your storytelling, and your determination to help others through the obstacles you have had to overcome. Thank you.

  - Joshua and Kathleen

Haley Moritz, Shirley McKay, Allison McLean, Don Zieman, Barbara Anschuetz, Marcellus Wiradharma, Venessa Kerman, Aaron Polka, Bradley McKay, Kathy Gosney, Anne Reade, Debbie Russell, Janice Nicholson, Diane Ashby, Fred Zierau, Jackie Arenburg, James Morton, Graham Frampton, Yuliya Demish, Richard Scott, Roberto Rongo, Bobbi Buchanan, Bonnie Crinnion, Angie Dorey, Trudie Shumaker, Brenda Thompson-Woodworth, and Laura Davies.

# Table of Contents

**Introduction** .................................................................................. v
  - Joshua Rivedal and Kathleen Myre

**The Truth behind the Smile** ........................................................ 1
  - Jean-Guy Poirier

**Death's Curse** .............................................................................. 5
  - Lee J. Plummer

**Breaking the Unwritten Rule of Silence:**
**A Firefighter's Story** ................................................................... 9
  - John Arenburg

**I Am Not "Broken"** ...................................................................... 13
  - Grant Bourne

**About Betrayal** ............................................................................ 17
  - Linda Green

**Gratitude for PTSD** .................................................................... 21
  - Marie-Julie Cosenzo

**Edge of Darkness** ....................................................................... 25
  - Matt McGregor

**Thank You, Monica** .................................................................... 29
  - Myles Hall

**What the Hell is Happening to Me?** ......................................... 33

- Paula Elias

**To the Brink and Back** ...... 37
- Rob Leathen

**I'm Sorry We Couldn't Save You** ...... 41
- Sarah Roselli

**The "Aha" Moment** ...... 45
- Syd Gravel

**Echoes of the Mind** ...... 49
- Tim Grutzius

**Through Darkness Beauty Grows** ...... 53
- Tracy Eldridge

**The Nothing that Never Happened** ...... 57
- William Young

**The Guy with All the Cool Stories** ...... 61
- Carl Waggett

**The Value of Kindness** ...... 65
- Brad McKay

**What's the Worst that Could Happen?** ...... 69
- Angela Ponting

**I'm Just a Volunteer** ...... 73
- Andrew Moritz

**Our Darkest Nights are Our Truest Gifts** ...... 77
- Terrance Kosikar

# Your i'Mpossible Story ...... 81

Author Biographies...................................................83

Also by Joshua Rivedal...................................................93

# Lemonade is Back...
# Now Sugar Free!

IF YOU KNOW ME, Josh, professionally or personally, you know that I love a good story. Stories connect us, change us, and inspire us to do more and be better. Stories often allow us to assess our current circumstances and can validate both our triumphs as well as our tribulations and also provide us a template of sorts so we can reframe if needed and turn the lemons in our life into lemonade.

My own story truly starts with my grandfather, Haakon, a veteran of the Second World War with the Royal Air Force and the Royal Canadian Air Force. He joined in 1941 and at the outset of his service, he served as a tail gunner on the back of bomber planes. At one point he even got shot down while flying a mission over Germany. Much of what I know about him is not through the very spotty information I got as a child, but more so from press clippings I sought out as an adult. After the war, I discovered that my grandfather was afflicted by both untreated mental illness and posttraumatic stress (back in his day, it was referred to as "shell shock"). A little more than twenty years after the war in Germany ended, he died by suicide because of the lack of resources, the unacceptability in speaking out about his trauma, and the dearth of peer support.

I'm convinced that if Haakon had more support he may have lived, and I may have gotten to know him when I was a child.

Many in the world who have supported others through emergency services, armed services, first responder work, front-line caregiving and more; and yet when these brave and noble people need support for themselves, they are denied or they have been conditioned to stay silent and "push through it" or pick themselves up by the bootstraps because they are supposed to be the strong ones so that other people can lean on them. This kind of thinking needs to go the way of the dodo. We need to start planting seeds from an early age and through continuing education courses that asking for help is one of the strongest things a person can do. Carers and those who serve cannot be of help if they are depleted or unable to lean on others for support.

I am so grateful for the authors in this book—firefighters, first responders, veterans of armed services; people who have helped others by making service their career. These brilliant people have been through a lot and have seen a great deal of trauma, some even afflicted with moral injury; and yet here they are again, working hard on themselves and working through the trauma while fighting the stigma and showing the world, "I've been through hell and can manage the burns; you can too." They are making it acceptable to ask for and receive help, and by doing so they are once again making the world a better place to live in. Thank you to these twenty incredible human beings.

Before we continue, I would be remiss if I didn't allow my co-author and co-curator to say a few words.

* * *

Like Josh, I believe in the power of storytelling to learn from or understand the life of another. I've recently become a Florida Certified Recovery Peer Specialist; a person with a significant life-altering experience who shares their story with others to give them hope during their own recovery. Fifteen years ago, I was diagnosed with depression and anxiety.

In January of 2019, I met Carl Waggett, a fellow peer, with lived experience as a firefighter with PTSD. I saw that Carl's story was making a difference in the lives of fellow first responders and it motivated me to find others in the community who were openly sharing their stories as well.

I do not have a first responder, emergency services, or military background but my passion to help others, end stigma, and prevent suicide was all the fuel I needed to take on this project. I know what it is like to feel alone and to perceive myself as weak. The voice of suicidal ideation has whispered in my ear and convinced me that ending my life would lead me to the eternal peace I so desperately wanted. Thankfully I got the help I needed before it was too late.

First responders, emergency service personnel, and military members face the elements every day to protect us and keep us safe. The mental pain of PTSD, anxiety, and depression plague their communities. Pushing it to the side or denying it exists is not a sound solution. Asking for help is one of the bravest things to do but the fear of stigma allows the code of silence to remain strong.

The twenty authors in this book are ready to step out of the shadows and shine a light on this issue to help those fighting this internal battle on their own. I have immeasurable respect for each of them as they rise up to bring about change as a means to save lives.

\* \* \*

What else do you need to know? Each chapter is one thousand words or less; each is a true story and is authored by a real person. The subject matter is about overcoming a big obstacle and how each person managed in the aftermath.

It is my and every author's hope that the stories in this book provide hope, healing, and connectivity.

Without further ado, I present to you the twenty incredible authors of *The i'Mpossible Project: Lemonade Stand Volume 3*.

# i
## The Truth Behind the Smile
### Jean-Guy Poirier

LIKE MOST OTHER PEOPLE with PTSD, changes in behavior along with isolated incidents of anger and rage were simply "put off" as possibly being tired or irritated. It wasn't until I had an "aha" moment back in late 2016 that I began to realize this was not an isolated event and my life was changing before my very own eyes.

I began my career as a volunteer firefighter in February 2005 in a small, rural community in Southeastern Ontario. Like most other newbies, things began on a high note, and life within the department was nothing like I'd experienced before. I jumped in with both feet and took on the role like I was born to be in that position. Calls came and went, and life moved on. Looking back on my career I can't pinpoint any particular incident that may have caused my PTSD therefore it was diagnosed and attributed to consecutive exposure to traumatic events. I could get into the specifics of calls and events but that doesn't change anything about my PTSD. What does change the PTSD is what you decide to do with yourself and how you approach your symptoms on a daily basis.

In the summer of 2015, I began to feel separated from the department, like I didn't belong anymore. Calls were getting tougher to process and were lingering around in my mind longer and longer. At this time, I was unknowingly beginning to isolate myself from the department as part of my symptoms with PTSD. In February of 2016, I resigned with the volunteer department unaware of the real reason behind it; simply chalking it up to my own insecurities and thoughts.

As 2016 progressed I began to experience many symptoms that became harder to deal with. My anger and rage were becoming more pronounced. One morning after having difficulty at home, I was traveling to work when I had an "aha" moment. At that point, I realized that I was changing as a person and I couldn't point to any particular reason why. I made an appointment to see my doctor in late 2016 where I was asked a series of questions that led to a discussion about post-traumatic stress disorder. My doctor was hesitant to diagnose and referred me to a mental health professional. The realization of this horrible disorder came to fruition in May 2017 when I was formally diagnosed. The therapy began slowly at first only hitting on struggles at that time. It was shortly after this that I began to encounter difficulties at home and work. Everyday procedures and routines were becoming more difficult to deal with and I found myself falling deeper into a battle within my own mind. This is a battle that hopefully, most people will never experience but this somehow landed me into the hospital because I began struggling with suicidal ideations. My initial thoughts after I checked myself into the hospital was that this was going to be a one- or two-day visit and things would turn around quickly. That didn't go as planned and I began to realize that my life had changed forever, and I was now going to have to deal with these symptoms every day. During my stay in the hospital, I decided that I wasn't going to sit around and take it. I needed to do something and find other people with PTSD so I could engage and learn more about this disorder and how to deal with it daily.

In September of 2017, I started a Facebook page entitled PTSD The Truth Behind The Smile; the goal of this was to serve as an outlet for myself and others to gain more knowledge about the disorder and to help each other as peer supporters. The page continued through 2017 and so did my struggles. That same year I saw myself separate from my marriage, lose my job of fifteen years, and move out into my own place.

During 2018 I saw many personal struggles, but the page continued. I started to notice that many people who were diagnosed did not come from an emergency profession background. This gave me an idea and I put my plan into action. I began the first PTSD Peer Support in my city and opened it up to anyone with PTSD. This was a huge step outside of my comfort zone but knowing that it was of such importance to others gave me the push I needed. The program and group saw tremendous growth and soon started to receive interest from other cities in the surrounding areas. In May 2019, I opened a second group in a neighboring city. The push to succeed has also presented me with opportunities that I never imagined possible. Facebook Live posts, radio airtime, news articles, and podcasts have all become a part of my advocacy and it's humbling to see how important this program is to others. The program/group will now be expanding into two other cities in fall 2019.

The success of this program is owed entirely to my surrounding support circle as well as the group members who make it all possible. You know who you are, and I will forever be in your debt. Keeping me strong and showing me how important it is to keep going has made me into the man I have become since being diagnosed with PTSD.

I would like to stress the importance of making the most of what you are presented with in life. When I was faced with this diagnosis I could have sat around and let it control me. But you can choose to be productive rather than let it take over your life. There is a little saying that I tend to repeat, "I have PTSD; PTSD doesn't have me." So, when you fall in life, get up, dust yourself off, and make the most of your situation.

# Death's Curse

## Lee J. Plummer

FOUR MONTHS INTO MY DEPLOYMENT, as the missiles flew across the sky, falling in various places on base, the sirens screamed the sound of danger approaching, telling us to get to bunkers. This was just a glimpse of my life. My days consisted of being a driver, and sometimes a gunner in Afghanistan, moving from one base to another. Sometimes down rigorous roads or up steep hillsides through the mountains of Afghanistan and small villages made from clay and straw, with no clear signs of electricity; all the while doing this during the darkness of night and sometimes during the scorching daylight.

In this time, I had seen, heard, smelled, and feared death, wondering if I would ever make it home. As war starts to consume you, you try to find a way out. My way out was going to be my M4 rifle. It could have been so easy, sitting there in my room, alone, with no one to interrupt me—eight clips, thirty rounds in each one of the 5.56 rounds. Granted I would only need one to take the pain away, and at this point in my life, I had no God by my side and no family. I had no support but myself to make a choice; life or death.

We lose twenty-two veterans a day to suicide. We hear about it, but we choose not to believe it until it becomes our issue. It's not that we don't have support or someone to call, it's that the time we have alone can be our most vulnerable point. It's as if once left alone, we get locked in a box with all the tools needed to give up. It becomes a mental battle. Do we choose life or death? Do we keeping driving on or do we kill the engine?

Many people only see the external, but not the internal. Whether it's my dreams, lack of sleep, depression, anxiety, anger and so much more, it all stems from my memories. You can't erase my mind or my thoughts and experiences. This is the problem because whether it's a year after the trauma or ten years when you hear a boom, it takes you back. When you see a flash, it takes you back. There are so many triggers that bring back memories, and every day is different. If it's an off day for you, it can throw you into an episode—sometimes small, sometimes big, sometimes it progresses throughout the day, week, or even month. The memories are what makes this battle everlasting.

Three days in country and I saw the aftermath of a VBIED (vehicle-borne improvised explosive device) while in an IED (improvised explosive device) training class. It was as if it were yesterday, standing there seeing two locals outside the wire walking to a spot in front of us, not quite knowing what they were doing until they stopped. Then one of them laid a flannel shirt down on the ground. The two men picked up the torso of the man who bombed the base. There were no arms, no legs, and no head on this torso from what we could see. They picked up this body, laid it in a shirt, wrapped it up, threw it over their back, then walked away as if nothing happened. If that doesn't tell you this isn't a game, I don't know what does, because this image is burnt into my brain and will forever trap apart of myself in the desert.

One night I was heading to the chow hall like I did every night, except I pushed it off this night due to getting caught up in a conversation with my roommate. Thankfully, I did because I originally had planned on leaving thirty minutes early. The walk alone took ten minutes. But on my way to eat, I heard a sound which I can only describe as a weapon misfiring, then a boom with the sound of something hitting metal. A missile had hit the roof of the chow hall. The roof deflected most of it, but what had made it through, killed a twenty-two-year-old kid in the Army, and a piece of scrap metal hit one of our senior chiefs in his neck. Everyone else either took cover or ran for cover until it was safe to help or get help. This one affected me because if I would have left when I wanted to, I might not be here today. I would have been somewhere in that galley eating, at the mercy of flying metal with the force of death behind it. There were plenty of other close calls, but this was just one of many incidences. It was the way of life during war.

Death is now our minds from the nightmares of everything we have seen and experienced firsthand accompanied by the fear of dying and never coming home. I often have thoughts of dying and what I would do in my final moments of life. How would I say my final words to my beautiful wife, my loving daughter, and my smart boy? What would I say?

I feel as though I have a glimpse or an idea of how it will happen. Death is a recurring theme within a veteran's mind, whether it be the past, present, or future. It's not that we want to die, it's just a part of us now. But we would gladly lay our lives down for the people and country we love, so they may live a life of freedom. Isn't that what we do for love? We sacrifice.

# Breaking the Unwritten Rule of Silence: A Firefighter's Story

## John Arenburg

**W**HEN I WAS NINETEEN, I joined the volunteer fire service in my community. Barely out of high school, I lacked the knowledge and experience that many of the veteran firefighters had. Being young and naive, the scenario I had envisioned in my mind's eye and the reality of helping others were two different things.

My limited life experience conjured up fantasies, not unlike that of a superhero movie. We as firefighters make order out of chaos, always resulting in the "everyone would live happily ever after scenario." Shortly after jumping on the rig for the first time,

I learned that this internal script I had written was, like that of superhero movies, a work of fiction.

Not long after I joined the service, my superhero fantasy was all but shattered as I responded to my first tragic fire call, a fatality in a structure fire. This incident would lay the foundation for my future mental health crisis. Consequently, the accumulation of so many fatal and near-fatal incidents that I responded to in my fifteen-year career, built up like carbon monoxide, manifesting itself in the form of post-traumatic stress disorder, major depressive disorder, and generalized anxiety disorder.

The volunteer fire service is rich with tradition; one of its oldest is an unwritten rule. You do not talk about how you're feeling inside regardless of how each run is affecting you. So, my psychological scrapes and bruises were repeatedly assaulted until they became cuts; slowly leeching in were symptoms of numbness, nightmares, and disassociation.

While in the course of my duties, attempting to mitigate or prevent death and destruction, I brought these symptoms along with me. The numbness and disassociation were amplified while on scene. Of course, I didn't understand them at the time. I could just "feel" something. At first how I felt during and after a call slowly dissipated. After a week passed, I would feel normal again.

What I failed to see was that these feelings didn't dissolve into thin air but rather, they embedded themselves deep within my unconscious and waited for the next tragic layer to arrive on top of the next. Silenced by stigma, that of "manning up," it allowed every critical incident to fester. Before I knew it, I was constantly at war with my inner self. As time went on, I became more irritable, more easily startled, and an unexplainable sadness settled over me like an early morning fog. This sadness, seemingly out of the blue, manifested itself as anger; another side effect of not being able to talk about the damage being done inside. The pervasive silence was harmful, and the fire service denied me the opportunity to seek the help I clearly needed. Because of that, I couldn't even identify what was happening to me. In those days, I had mistaken my body's warnings of impending danger as normal. Now, I have come to understand that silence truly is a killer.

In my fifteenth year, my manly silence got to me. Feelings as they relate to critical incidents finally overwhelmed me to the degree where I knew in my heart that it was time to close the bay doors for the last time. Still undiagnosed, the storms of illness roared inside me every day, making it more and more difficult to navigate through my world. So invasive were these feelings, that in the last few years as a firefighter I began to seek out professional help. Therapy was like a relief valve for all the pent-up pain that I was experiencing. I will always be happy that I showed the same amount of courage to help myself that I displayed when helping others. Breaking the silence that was eating away my entire being saved my life.

Inside, I felt that leaving the fire service would help by minimizing my anxiety, alleviate my sadness, and offload some of the everyday pain that had hitched a ride for the best part of my adult life. I was hopeful that this would make my feelings manageable enough to cope, thus making it easier to live my life. For a time, it proved to be successful.

I felt a certain amount of safety no longer being a firefighter because I felt that the odds of being part of another tragedy were extremely small. This allowed me to stay connected to the world and gave me the strength to conquer the storms forever off in the distance, tearing round in my head. I thought my conclusion was sound. After all, I had never had to take part in an emergency because I was no longer an emergency service worker.

Only a few short years after leaving the fire service, the notion that I would never take part in an emergency proved to be yet another fantasy. It was the evening of Thanksgiving, two years after I had left the service. I was attending dinner at my aunt's when a gentleman suddenly expired on the front step of her apartment building. Like the days of old, I went into autopilot and tried to medically assist this man who could not have been more than thirty. That day, the floodgates holding back every tragic moment I had been a part of busted wide open leaving me in the most severe state of this disassociation. It was as though I was there, but I was not. It rendered me incapable of assisting him in any way. I simply stood over him. There's little else I remember.

Now, with PTSD, confirmed, I am doing all I can to win my life back. On worker's compensation because of its severity, I use this time to help not only myself but others who remain in the shadows, afraid of the stigma. My life on pause, I am proving that hiding and denying will have very real consequences. There's no shame in mental pain. Please, seek the help you need.

# I Am Not "Broken"
## Grant Bourne

I DIDN'T KNOW THAT I WAS BROKEN "…I felt "fine." But here the military counselor was telling me that I had posttraumatic stress disorder, adjustment disorder, anxiety, depression, survivor's guilt, and anger management issues. And even though I had been sober for over seven years, I was being told that I am still an alcoholic.

It all made sense, but I was a Marine. That is all normal, right? So now we get to figure out where all of this came from. Or do we?

In 2006 I was a sergeant (E-5) in the Marine Corps. I was sent to Pennsylvania as a Marine Corps recruiter. Lucky me, I had a freshly promoted gunnery sergeant (E-7) who had also just taken over the recruiting substation as the boss. He was a narcissist, pathological liar, and all-around bad soul. Needless to say, my three years of recruiting were challenging because of him.

The second person who I enlisted into the Marines was amazing. A mechanic at heart who had just finished training to become a BMW technician. He was soft-spoken and smart. He had this smirk that I will never forget. He was a few years older than the average person who walked into my office, but he was dead set on being a Marine. He wanted to be an infantryman.

I was a helicopter mechanic. I couldn't understand how this smart, big-hearted guy wanted to be a grunt. I did my best to talk him out of it.

This young man would go to basic training at Paris Island, earn the title of U.S. Marine, finish infantry training, and get assigned to his unit only to find out that he would soon be deploying. That was all fine because that is what he wanted. So, he and his girlfriend had a small wedding and started planning their formal wedding that would take place a while after his return from deployment.

His deployment came and went, and he was back in the States. His deployment indeed changed him, as did some other screwed up situations once he got home.

His wife headed home for a visit with family and to finish up some of the wedding planning. called his brother and father and talked with them for a while. He called his wife again and all seemed well. But after hanging the phone up he lost his battle with his demons.

Did I truly try my best to talk him out of being a rifleman? No. Maybe in my state of mind at the time, I did. At the point in my life when he enlisted, I was fighting depression, anxiety, sleep and other medical issues, and alcohol abuse. I was drinking a fifth or more of Jack Daniels daily.

On November 4th, 2007, I drank half a fifth of vodka and over half a fifth of Jack on an empty stomach. I was in alcohol counseling at the time and had a meeting the next day too! Right before bed that night I decided that the leftover quesadilla in the fridge was a good idea. Sober me looks back and realizes that was a horrible idea!

I have been sober since November 5th, 2007. I walked into my counselor's office that morning and told her, "I am done coming here. More importantly, I am done drinking"

She replied with the same thing that she would tell me or even the group. "You will never be sober without my help and you will never be strong enough to do this without me!"

I left after a few colorful, loud, and angry words for her. One mile from my house was the bar that everyone knew me at. That drive home was the hardest I have ever had to make, but the person who honked at me while I was parked at a green light may have saved my life that day.

A little over a year later, I was struggling with my relationship, work, in the middle of planning a wedding, and then I heard about the loss of an amazing Marine and rifleman.

July 7th, 2009 was a rough day for me. I was driving my Jeep Wrangler while at work. I indeed was goofing off while "on the clock." I got a phone call from my "interesting" boss. It was a ridiculous call that wasn't needed.

That call was the straw that broke the camel's back.

Between my fiancée at the time, work, and life in general the stress and anger won. I quit. I gave up. I slammed on the brakes in my Jeep, yanked the wheel over to the shoulder, slammed it into park, pulled out my pistol, placed it on my head, placed my finger on the trigger disengaging the safety, and closed my eyes.

At that split second, I heard the screams in my head of the young Marine's wife and mother from when I was at his funeral.

I took a deep breath, lowered my pistol from the side of my head, and unfortunately never stopped pulling the trigger. In the end, all is well, but the fourteen-inch titanium rod that held my right femur together for about eighteen months sits on my nightstand as a reminder that no matter how bad things may seem, they can and indeed will get better.

I have been at my lowest. Now I do my best to let others know that they are not broken. That its normal to not always be "okay" and that even when things get tough, they can still end up amazing. Regardless of what anyone says, you are not broken! You are on your own unique journey. Please remember that you are loved, you have value, and you have purpose! Please do not give up!

# About Betrayal
## Linda Green

"I CAN'T IMAGINE HOW THAT that must feel..." The false platitudes of support burn deeply. Here's the thing, though. I don't have to imagine it. I've been there.

My journey with post-traumatic stress began in 2015 when I looked at a co-worker's burned hands. He went to the hospital. I stayed on the incident for another eighteen hours, witnessing the conflagration known as the Valley Fire.

Not many people know I was symptomatic within an hour of seeing my friend's horrific injuries. I was confused by the tidal wave of claustrophobia that slammed into me unannounced. The insomnia showed up within a week. The Incredible Hulk, also known as raging anger, was evident within a couple of months.

By the time I was diagnosed with PTSD several months later, I was paranoid and had a startle response, even while walking the relative safety of headquarters. When I finally felt compelled to tell my immediate supervisor about my injury, I felt betrayed by his callous remarks. I was too angry and too scared to see the truth. It took another couple of years to get there.

Hopefully, what I'm about to say will help shorten the duration of your own sense of betrayal. The bureaucracy of a department is not designed to help people like you and me recover from a post-traumatic stress injury. It's designed to buy equipment, staff shifts, and track expenditures for a budget cycle. No more. No less.

The insurance agencies are driven by policies and actuarial tables. They only cover what the state allows them to cover. Some states do not recognize PTSD as a work-related injury. Fortunately, that's changing, but it is still an obstacle to overcome.

The people who promote the brotherhood and sisterhood of the department mean well. The sense of comradery that working in public safety provides can't be beat by any other government agency, save the military establishment. But the people who wear the uniform are as ill-equipped to support you as the bureaucracy. Few recruit academies expend more than an hour or two on the topic of mental health, and robust peer support teams are few and far between.

Betrayal is really just failed expectations. You expected support that you didn't get. I know that was true for me. But was it?

One person didn't support me. I focused too much energy in that direction. I was angry. Livid actually—until I realized that there was nothing I could about that situation. Staying angry blocked my recovery, so I had to let it go until later. I focused on what I needed to focus on, and that was me.

Nothing was off the table where my recovery was concerned, and that included talking about that vision that kept dancing in my head. I built my own support team. The first person outside of immediate family and the medical profession that I contacted was a retiree I knew who had fought the same demons.

I finally started to attend some AA meetings at the suggestion of my friend. It provided a social structure outside of work, and I was reasonably certain of anonymity. I wasn't convinced that I was an alcoholic until my withdrawal symptoms extended beyond three days.

Few people at work knew of my injury. The ones who did know were carefully selected. Not everyone is worthy of that knowledge. Your support team needs to be small. They may not come from your normal source of connections, and that's okay. You need a fresh and honest perspective that they can provide.

The sole job of your support team is to help you stay within the guard rails of your recovery pathway. If they are enabling your destructive behavior, they don't belong on your team. Sometimes it helps to know that you are not alone on your recovery pathway. That others have walked the same path ahead of you. That others are holding up a guiding light of hope for you to follow.

Recovery is possible. It's hard work. Being a first responder is hard work too. You already know how to tap into that inner strength you possess to get the job done. Tap into it again for this job. As others believed in me, I believe in you. Work on your recovery with everything you can muster. It's worth it.

# Gratitude for PTSD
## Marie-Julie Cosenzo

I STARTED PACKING AWAY MY traumas as a six-year-old in the aftermath of my grandfather's fatal collision with a train. As the years went by, I kept tucking away my traumas. When I became a paramedic, I continued witnessing pain and suffering, doing the job I loved for eight glorious years. On October 3$^{rd}$, 2015, the night I responded to the suicide of a teenager, I knew something had changed—not just because I cried uncontrollably in my truck. I couldn't file that call away like the others. My cabinet burst open, flinging all my traumas in the air. What was once put away for life came out in a flurry of sounds, images, smells, and feelings. I frantically tried to shove them back in their box, but there were too many. When that shift ended, I took off my uniform for the last time. Shortly after, I was diagnosed with complex trauma post-traumatic stress disorder (C-

PTSD), major depressive disorder, generalized anxiety disorder, and obsessive-compulsive disorder.

I had a choice: I could give in to my suicidal urges and end my pain, or fight. During a stint of in-patient treatment, another resident told me how as a toddler, his mother had ended her life and that it still haunted him. That day I decided that even at my most suicidal, I would stay alive for my son. He is the only person for whom I am truly irreplaceable.

After about six months of lying about going to work to extended family and friends, I decided to come clean, 2016-style: I posted a long-winded message on Facebook. I worried about receiving negative messages, but I got love and support instead. I even had people share their own stories of pain with me. I felt privileged to be trusted with these secrets. It was then that I chose to share my challenges, victories, and coping strategies more openly and regularly. There is no shame in having mental illnesses!

In the middle of my court battle to get coverage from my province's workplace and safety board, I had my driver's license suspended because of my special class for driving an ambulance and my cocktail of mental illnesses. After licking my wounds for a few days, I went to the press. I thought that if it happened to me, this had surely happened to other first responders as well. My local member of provincial government, who had publicly shared her own struggles with depression, came to my rescue. Within six weeks, I was informed I could get behind the wheel again, and that my new license was in the mail. Afterwards, I was contacted by several other paramedics who were in the same situation. I was thrilled to be able to guide them towards reinstatement.

I was once again able to help strangers.

Around the same time, I was "found" by the facilitator of a peer support group for struggling first responders. He had listened to a podcast where I talked about my experiences as a paramedic, and about my license suspension. I was relieved to find others like me: same weird habits, same hatred for public spaces, same broken coping strategies. As time went on, group became an important part of my recovery. The more meetings I went to and the more blog posts went up, the more people told me how my path to recovery gave them hope for their own.

Again, I was helping strangers.

During my second year of being off work, I had become increasingly isolated. During my suspension, I had grown accustomed to doing my errands accompanied by my husband or my parents. I could barely leave the house alone and would frequently have panic attacks in public places. Shortly after this started happening, I was diagnosed with agoraphobia. When I won my court case, my diagnoses were officially recognized as workplace injuries. I would be compensated for the lost wages and have some of the thousands of dollars spent on psychotherapy, massage therapy, and medication reimbursed. Testifying was a terrible process that nearly made me kill myself, but I didn't want to let them win.

I was rewarded with a new psychologist and an occupational therapist. Together, we made a list of places to go so I could regain my independence. After all, I was the toddler who insisted on holding her own hands while walking downtown with her parents! We started with the basics, like leaving my car once we got to the grocery store, working our way to entering a hospital. With every level I beat (it was like a video game where every step was increasingly difficult), I gained more self-confidence. I was even able to have a surgery that I had put off because I feared the mandatory overnight stay. My numerous victories in exposure therapy allowed me to do something scarier than going to Costco: I booked a three-week trip to India with my best friend. That trip was filled with magical moments. From seeing the Taj Mahal up close to meditating on the beach during a Goan sunset, I felt my soul being rewarded and soothed for all the hard work and pain I had endured during the previous years.

Shortly after my return to reality, I began EMDR (eye movement desensitization and reprocessing) therapy with my psychologist. It is gruelling and horrible, but it is helping me to properly "digest" my traumas, allowing me to truly move forward.

Throughout my crises and victories, my family has been there for me. Every encouraging word, text, and hug have propped me up so I can keep fighting. I have taught my kids that when faced with a challenge, we fight. My husband has shown me what true love means: he has done more for me than he realizes, and for that, I am incredibly grateful.

Unconditional love is has allowed me to be grateful for PTSD: without it, I would not know how strong I am.

# Edge of Darkness
## Matt McGregor

I HAD ONLY BEEN SOBER A month. I wanted to die, and I had a plan. It was Christmas and I was in utter darkness. I was an out-of-control alcoholic. Whilst I had accepted my drinking habits had morphed into a life-threatening indulgence, my newly embraced sobriety had not yet pulled me out of the woods. I was still very lost, and even though I had my young son, Carter, the support of the fire department and Steve, who was my best friend and business partner; I was alone, and I wasn't confident I'd remain sober. I didn't know whether I had the strength to overcome my demons—that I wouldn't succumb to the cravings for the numbness I so deeply yearned for to escape my reality.

I began to prepare my final act. It wasn't the first time I'd made plans to end my life, but this time it was different, I was accepting my fate and my reality. I was tired. Christmas was looming and I wasn't looking forward to it. I began to dread the reality that I would be alone at Christmas—so depressing. I didn't believe I had the strength to make it past Christmas Eve, so I began to prepare for the end of my own private hell. I knew it involved one last drowning in alcohol, a lot of vodka, many tears, and carbon monoxide.

In the days leading up to Christmas, Steve insisted that I spend time with him and his family. But I knew I had no place with them. As the Christmas break approached, I spent my evenings either alone, or with my young son whom I was about to abandon in death. Even the company of my own son wasn't releasing me from my insurmountable decline. I hated everything about my life. I felt a failure on so many levels. I wasn't fit to be a father, a husband, or even a friend.

My end was approaching, and I began to prepare my thoughts for my letter. I assumed I'd be forgotten anyway, so it didn't matter. My son would live on. He'd still live a good life with his mother and her family. She'd likely remarry, and Carter would have a stepfather. He would need a father figure a thousand times better than me. I had already seen how my behaviour was hurting and confusing him. He'd be better off without me. And moving away wasn't an option.

My final hour was literally days away, but the universe had other ideas—my world shifted, and my plans went sideways. It seemed the world reached out and asked *me* for help. I was called to address a serious situation at a ski resort. An equipment malfunction had potentially filled an entire building with carbon monoxide, threatening the lives of its population of holiday skiers—a life-or-death emergency relating to the very gas I'd planned to use to end my own life.

Carbon monoxide suddenly became my nemesis, and as a highly experienced gas fitter, well-versed in the hazards associated with gas-burning equipment, I was the man qualified to meet the challenge. The incident had the potential to seriously harm or kill dozens of people, and it was now my task to solve their very serious problem, and at the busiest time of the season. Despite my personal difficulties, I loved my job. I knew the resort's emergency was likely due to poor maintenance and it would now be my mission, and mine alone, to fix their equipment in order for them to safely operate their business and keep their clientele safe. I ended up working nearly seven days straight to resolve the crisis. I made the company a good amount of revenue doing so. I was distracted and now I had a purpose; I had a new light in which to see the world. I had managed to escape the sadness of the Christmas season and it was all I'd needed, at least at that point.

They had needed *me*, and I had the experience to manage the situation. As Christmas passed, I began thinking beyond suicide. I started gaining momentum. And in another turn of fate, a second corporation on that same hill had a complete failure of their entire gas operating system. On New Year's Day, I was once again tasked with solving a vital utility failure, this time for a small town. And with that, we began to discuss plant maintenance work for them. They actually asked us if we were interested in purchasing their utility. Wow. What was happening here?

And so, as the weeks wore on, Steve and I kept doing what we had been doing, grinding it out, trying to make our business a success. We continued to communicate with the utility in the hope that our dreams may come to fruition, perhaps potentially purchase this utility, but in the end, it wasn't to be. I ended up moving on from the business and taking a well-suited position as a consultant in the same industry.

And here I am—happy, successful, and finding peace in writing about my journey, which is now mostly rewarding.

What this story doesn't share is its subplot. At the time of these events, I was a seasoned volunteer firefighter in a very busy fire department nearby. A firefighter's life can be one of extreme trauma and addiction that puts the foretold near-death experience to shame. This is my story. Because what was to come in the next two years would test my will to survive to the extreme.

At the time of writing, I have navigated the darkest of darkness on my healing journey. In my service as a firefighter, I have witnessed and experienced the most horrific anguish and suffering imaginable. But what's even more compelling is that during my descent into hell to repair what I thought was line-of-duty trauma, I discovered I had been suppressing my childhood trauma that had begun at birth.

# Thank You, Monica
## Myles Hall

"I CAN'T DO IT... I JUST CAN'T," I said out loud. It was an all too familiar phrase I had said to myself the past year or so. Frustrated at my lack of ability to focus, I placed my head in my hands and started crying. The whole ritual wreaked further havoc on my confidence to do anything. I pulled myself together after a few minutes, but it didn't matter. The damage was done. My latest assault on my self-worth was as a result of a discussion that I had with a friend about PSTD—my affliction with it from my twenty years as a member of the Royal Canadian Mounted Police. The advice I was given, and the reason for my mini-breakdown, was to contact veteran's affairs and apply for a disability pension; something that would help out greatly given that maintaining regular work had become one of my stressors, "life" and the cost of it doesn't stop just because you don't "feel good." This stress led to triggers, which led to PTSD symptoms, which led to further stressors. I was getting tired of the mental merry-go-round. But what is it that I just couldn't do? Think...concentrate...focus, all impossibilities.

As ridiculous as it sounds, I felt overwhelmed by the federal administrative task that lay ahead, I had no idea of what it consisted of much less how to fill out all the forms. It didn't matter that I had done this kind of thing for twenty years, that I was no stranger to filling in data and checking off boxes. All I knew now, was that concentrating on anything was difficult, but having to figure out complex instructions...well...that was damn near impossible.

Fast forward to my next psychology appointment. I brought up what happened with my therapist and it turned into the focal point of our discussion for the session. By the end, I was ready to contact veterans affairs. "Overwhelmed" had just been reduced to "nervous." After a quick phone call, I was advised that I would be contacted by a representative. *This ought to be good*, I thought, planning for the worst-case scenario. *I'll probably hear from them in a year.*

A week or so later my cell phone rang. It was an odd number that I didn't recognize. "Hello, may I speak to Myles."

"Yes, speaking."

"Hi Myles, this is Monica calling from veterans affairs. Do you have time to come and see me sometime this week? I'd like to talk to you about your application for disability pension."

After making an appointment, I ended the call and immediately my stress levels began to build. I was sure I'd get a good grilling from Monica who would no doubt ask all the right questions to deny my claim. Why the hell did I even start this process? What was I thinking?

My appointment finally came around and I found myself in the waiting room of the veterans affairs office in downtown Regina, Saskatchewan. A petite blonde-haired woman exited an office door and approached me.

"Myles...hi. I'm Monica, I'm glad you could make it in. Let's have a seat in my office," she said in a soft tone.

*Well, at least she doesn't appear intimidating*, I thought as I followed her into the room containing her desk.

"Myles, the first thing I want to tell you is that I work for you, not the government."

After a very pleasant back and forth conversation concerning my circumstances, one that lasted well into an hour, I found myself unusually comfortable. This "meeting" felt more like a therapy session. Monica was compassionate and understanding. I began to explain to Monica that I simply couldn't fill out all the paperwork and couldn't explain why. I told her that I felt like an idiot for even saying such a thing.

"Don't you worry about a thing Myles. I'll get everything all ready. You come see me when you can in a couple of days, and I'll help you fill it all out. I understand that even the simplest things can feel impossible."

I started to well up with emotion inside to the point where I could feel myself tearing up. Hearing Monica say those words was a total game-changer for me. Someone who "understands." I found myself becoming very thankful that I mustered up the courage to push forward with what I was sure would be an insurmountable task. It resulted in the blessing of a fantastic woman becoming involved in my life. "Thank you, Monica."

# What the Hell is Happening to Me?

## Paula Elias

I HAD CHEST PAINS, MIGRAINES, and high blood pressure. I was a nervous wreck. I didn't want to see anyone or go anywhere. I started online shopping—way too much. I began eating sugary, fatty, tasty carbs way too much. I woke up every night and couldn't fall back asleep. When I did sleep, I had such intense dreams I would eventually wake up with my chest pounding. I was afraid my kids would hurt themselves everywhere, doing anything. I could see the catastrophe happening in my mind's eye and it was horrible.

My biggest clue—had I been looking for clues to my problem instead of trying to just "handle" everything—was that I didn't want to go to work. I have always wanted to go to work. I'm a firefighter. I love my job. I decided a change of command, station, and truck would help. A fresh start to reenergize things. Nope. A few days off was all I needed. A break. Then a few more, then a few weeks. I'd be fine then. Nope and nope.

It was my brother who delicately suggested that I might be dealing with PTSD. What? No way. Absolutely not! That's for soldiers and victims of horrific crimes. I was just a firefighter who needed to find a way to suck it up a little more. However, I did do a little research. It explained everything, whether I wanted to admit it or not. The doctors subsequently agreed.

However, this diagnosis wasn't a relief by any means because it was my fault this had happened to me. I wasn't tough enough; I couldn't hack it. A female firefighter wimping out just like expected. I was humiliated. I didn't tell anyone I wasn't required to. I barely admitted it to myself. Because if I did, I would have to answer the question I thought I had known the answer to: who am I? I thought I was tough; both mentally and physically, could handle all that came my way. I was confident in the fact that I had earned my place on the truck and held my own. But wait, if I had PTSD, I could not be that person.

My confidence evaporated, I became more despondent, more depressed, developing MDD (major depressive disorder) to boot. I questioned everything about myself and my place in the world. All while blaming myself and feeling crushing shame. Nevertheless, this is not a story of hopelessness. My tale does not end here.

It is possible to fight your way back to enjoying a worthwhile life and maybe, dare I say, to becoming a better, more enlightened person than you were when all this crap started. Maybe "enlightened" is too strong a word, but certainly more knowledgeable, more understanding, and more accepting of who you are and what you are dealing with.

I don't have a magical panacea; I can only share what has worked for me. I count myself incredibly lucky to have met a therapist who not only specializes in emergency services but with whom I feel a strong connection. Without this trust and sense of comfort, I feel during our appointments, I would never have been able to open up the way I have; actually, much more than I thought I ever would. Slowly and carefully, she has helped me to see my problems, situations, and opinions in a new light. It is this perspective that has caused a shift in me—this was not something I did; this was something that happened to me. I am not weak because of it; I am stronger for choosing to fight through it.

I also participated (kicking and screaming) in a firefighter PTSD group that turned out to be an illuminating and bonding experience I'm very grateful for. Working with an occupational therapist has helped immensely as well. I see her as a kind of life coach, helping me get things in order and talking through insecurities and stressors though so they do not seem so daunting. The last piece of the recovery puzzle was finding the podcast Bunker Gear for Your Brain. I felt a connection to the host Carl right away. He was around the same age, had been on the job about as long, and had also developed cumulative PTSD. I didn't judge him or think him weak, so why did I think that of myself?

Let me wrap up by sharing this: I made dinner today—from scratch! I even went out and got the groceries myself. For most people, my former self-included, this is no big deal. A daily routine, which either loved or hated, is done, nonetheless. It's been three years since I've made a delicious meal for my family that consisted of more than grilled cheese, pasta, or pancakes. I couldn't be more thrilled. Laugh if you will, it doesn't bother me because I get the enormity of this common task. I have learned so much on this detour my life has taken. It's not important what people may think. I care more about how I feel. The debilitating shame has lessened its hold on me. I am more comfortable in my own skin and feel I'm armed with tools I can use to help me navigate life. Quite simply my perspective has changed.

Having lost so many things to PTSD for so long, I am happy to say I'm getting them back. A feat I never thought possible when my journey began. While I still have bad days, I do consider myself a work in progress. Although it's been no fairytale, I feel my story will have a happy ending.

# To the Brink and Back
## Rob Leathen

IN FEBRUARY 2019, I REALIZED that things weren't quite right with me. My wife, however, most definitely knew. I was having lots of arguments with my wife over the littlest of things—complete meltdowns saying hurtful nasty things that I wish I could take back. Each meltdown was followed by an inexplicable but incredible sense of calm, almost as if absolutely nothing had happened. My ego always told me I was in the right. At the time I didn't know that what I was experiencing were classic symptoms of severe PTSD and severe major depressive disorder—a realization that only came after a psychological assessment nearly four months later.

I have been a firefighter and first responder for the better part of twenty-seven years. In that timeframe, I've done and seen a lot. I've seen and heard things that the human brain was never meant to handle, things that stop your brain dead in its tracks as if a pause button were pressed. I've smelled things that I can never un-smell, those memories forever burned into my very being. I've "danced" with the fiery devil himself, and always lead, never allowing the devil to step on my toes. My ego was my dance coach. Not so surprising considering my career choice, PTSD and depression should almost have been expected but they weren't. I never expected it or saw it coming. I always figured it would have been some occupational cancer that "got" me. I wasn't too concerned though because my ego told me I didn't need to be.

During my mental health journey with PTSD and depression, like so many others, there have been many ups and downs. My ego kept telling me not to worry and that I could handle it all, after all, I was a firefighter. I've seen it all; I've done it all. There have been good days and bad days and some very dark days. The phrase "dark days" always puzzled me and I started to see it for what it was, the code phrase used to indirectly refer to the elephant in the room. Hell, let's not beat around the bush as some do. During those dark days, and one day in particular, I was suicidal.

In the early days of my rollercoaster mental health journey, I learned that physical pain has absolutely nothing on emotional pain. I'll gladly take a root canal with no numbing agent. I learned that sometimes emotional pain overwhelms you and makes you feel helpless and hopeless and desperate to escape that pain. Along with the distorted thought processes that accompany PTSD, you'll sometimes do anything to escape that pain. I made my decision; I knew what I was going to do. I didn't have a plan just yet, that was what the next couple of days were going to be for, to figure out the how and the when. Funny thing is my ego remained silent during those couple of days almost like a child that got caught doing something they weren't supposed to be doing. During those few days I came to realize that while stigma surrounding mental health still exists, the stigma surrounding suicide is ten times worse. Because I didn't want to burden my wife, daughter, and son with having to live with that stigma for the rest of their lives, I stepped back from the brink; from the point of no return. My ego was right there with me when I made that lifesaving decision but this time its voice sounded a little more like a whimper of defeat.

I started learning everything I could about my mental health gift; yes, I actually said gift. I learned about the symptoms, the physiology, and the psychology of PTSD and depression. I learned about meditation and yoga and something called polyvagal theory. I learned about coping strategies and self-soothing techniques. I even learned about what my window of tolerance was and how to be aware of exactly where I was within it. Who knew? Heck, I jokingly tell people that with the amount I've learned I am almost a full-fledged psychologist. Well...minus the multiple degrees and years of education but still pretty damn close!

I continue to go to weekly therapy and continue to make forward progress with my recovery. I'm slowly becoming a different person, a better person. With the guidance of my therapist, I've been able to take control of my PTSD symptoms and take control of the distorted thought processes governed by the cognitive distortions instilled in me by PTSD. I've been able to rid myself of many of the negative thoughts and beliefs I used to hold. I've also been able to rid myself of my ego. It was once my good friend helping to drive me to achieve things I didn't think I ever could, but now it is nothing but a recent memory of something that nearly cost me my life. Without my good friend "ego," I've been able to experience some post-traumatic growth. Without my ego, I've been able to take, what for many is a life-altering diagnosis, and turn it into something positive. As part of my healing journey, I now advocate for first responder mental health and educate other first responders. Who knows? Perhaps one day I'll even write about my story so that it can be included in a book...

# I'm Sorry We Couldn't Save You

## Sarah Roselli

**T**HOSE YOU LOSE STAY WITH YOU. It's haunting...

*To my first overdose victim.*

It wasn't even my shift. It wasn't even my night to work. But when "thirty-year-old female; possible overdose" toned out over the loudspeaker, the night chief looked at me and pleaded, "Can you come? In case she wakes up...it would be good to have a female there so she's more comfortable."

I gave a quick nod as I pulled on my job shirt and zipped up my boots. When we left the station, dispatch told us it was a possible CPR in progress, so we gathered our supplies: Narcan to reverse the effects of the drugs, an airway to keep your lungs open, a BVM to pump oxygen into your body, and an AED to restart your heart. It was our arsenal of weapons against death.

We pulled up to the scene, which was now swarmed with cops. "I think she's dead," muttered the detective.

We entered your apartment and danced over smashed beer cans, empty pill bottles, broken glass, and torn up newspapers, trying not to disturb the scene. I looked up and saw you laying on the couch. The first thing I noticed was how your legs were spread open; there was a blanket draped across the bend of your knees. My eyes worked their way up your body and saw one of your arms crossed over your stomach; the other was hanging off the couch as if it was grasping for help that came too late. You died reaching for someone, or maybe toward something.

Your mouth was opened as if you were crying out for help. When we tried to close your jaw, it wouldn't move. Your cells used up their last bit of energy to make your body stiff.

*This was the first sign of death. (rigor mortis)*

I put my hand to your neck in desperate search of a pulse beneath the tips of my fingers. I couldn't find one.

*This was the second sign of death. (lack of spontaneous circulation)*

When we rolled you on your side and lifted your shirt, we saw how the blood settled to your back. It stained your body different shades of white and purple, which followed the pattern of the wrinkled sheets beneath you. It had been a while since your blood was circulating.

*This was the third sign of death. (lividity)*

When the paramedics arrived, they pronounced you.

*Every time the clock turns 0204, I think of you.*

To the husband of my first overdose victim.

Dead bodies are weird right? They don't look like they're sleeping. I don't care how many books you've read and movies you've watched, the dead don't look peaceful. I know you couldn't even look at her; I saw how your eyes stayed fixed to the mess beneath our feet.

*I'm sorry you had to see her like that.*

It was just a fight. Husbands and wives fight. God, how could you have known this would happen? It wasn't your fault. You didn't do this to her. It wasn't your fault, but I know for the rest of your life, you will feel like it was. I know you'll replay all your lasts: last hug, last kiss, last tears, last fight, last words.

*Don't forget about all your firsts, too.*

When the police finish taking pictures, you'll clean up the empty vodka bottles, pick up the broken needles, and sweep up the shattered glass. You'll neatly fold the clean laundry she forgot to take out of the dryer and you'll try to match all the pairs of socks right this time. Maybe you'll empty the dishwasher even though it's your least favorite thing to do; even though it was always her job.

*I know the house will feel empty without her in it.*

I know we were called because of your wife, but we treated two victims today. I know you were upset with us for not doing more. You were pleading with us to use the arsenal of weapons we left at your front door. You pounded your fists against the walls and cursed us and a god up above as tears fell and stained your cheeks. I smelled the alcohol on your breath when we tried to pick your limp body off the floor; you had finally given into the grief.

*We did everything we could, but death settled in too quickly. I'm so sorry...*

We gathered the last of our supplies, obtained signatures from the officers standing guard at your doorstep, and pulled the sheet up over her face. The last thing we said to you before leaving was, "I'm sorry for your loss."

*We're told to say it, but what a dumb thing to say.*

I know part of you died with her. I know the idea of living in this world without her is unfathomable, but please promise you'll try. Try not to let the dishes pile up. Try to fold all of the laundry while it's still warm from the heat of the dryer. Try to pick your head up off the floor and look people in the eyes. Try to let the grief settle, and don't let the guilt stay too long.

*This isn't your fault.*

# The "Aha" Moment
## Syd Gravel

FRESH OUT OF COLLEGE, I experienced some traumatizing events. From being imprisoned as a suspected mercenary while surveying the countryside during the Frelimo Revolution in Mozambique and then surveying in Nigeria after the Biafran Civil war to becoming a police officer in Ottawa where I shot at my first robbery suspect with only two weeks on the job. I thought I had it all figured out.

Truth was, I was young and arrogant, and I didn't have a clue. I first noticed some difficulties after returning from Africa. I was uncomfortable being in large crowds. I had restless nights and abused alcohol almost daily. I started to isolate myself from everyone and everything.

Eight years into the job, my partner and I responded to a robbery call. It didn't go well. The end result—I fatally shot one of the suspects. I had every reason to believe he was armed and was about to use his gun, but he was unarmed. He was only trying to get rid of the money he had stuffed into his pants. I made a decision based on everything I saw and how I was trained.

Since that moment, there isn't a day that goes by I don't think about the horror of that decision. For more than thirty-two years now I wish that I hadn't been there. I continue to wonder if there will ever be an end to the remembering.

I didn't join the police to cause harm; I was raised wanting to help people, not kill them. I understood the concept of using force if necessary. But I never equated doing this part of the job with the personal and moral conflict it would create in me. The fatal use of force would cause me considerable suffering.

For months after the incident, I spent hours pacing the floors, night after night, most times in a drunken stupor, trying to logically work my way past the barrier that blocked my ability to understand why I was feeling the way I was. I kept going over the event, asking myself hundreds of times: Did I miss something? Did I react too quickly?

There was never an answer. No matter how justified the act to shoot was deemed to be, I felt broken inside. I couldn't figure out how to fix myself so I could stop thinking about what had happened. I eventually reached a dark and exhausting place where suicide seemed like the only option left. I had held on as long as I could.

My wife, however, saw that somewhere within the mess of a man that she now lived with was the man she loved. She wanted to find him in me again. But all my attempts to heal myself had failed so far. So, she stepped in and arranged for me to see a psychologist who specialized in the treatment of trauma.

After the first meeting, I trusted him and his approach and the journey to recovery began.

I finally realized I could no more fix my damaged brain than I could a broken bone. It took time and sometimes I would fall back, but never as far back as I had been. With every step forward, I became stronger. And with each of those steps, my wife walked along beside me.

Moving forward from a traumatic event can be difficult. The biggest issue I was dealing with was the ever-festering emotion of anger. Angry that I had to make a decision that cost a man his life. Angry that the job required it of me to be there. Angry that people saw me as a hero for doing what I had done.

I came to realize that the guy who was hurting me the most was me. Everyone else had moved on but me. Anger was the source of many of my problems. The question I then had to ask of myself was, "How much am I willing to damage my life to spite others?"

Dr. Jonathan Shay, a clinical psychiatrist with the U.S. Department of Veterans Affairs, defined moral injury as … "the damage done to one's conscience or moral compass when that person perpetrates, witnesses, or fails to prevent, acts that transgress their own moral and ethical values and codes of conduct." Becoming aware of this was my "aha" moment.

It is this moral injury that sometimes feeds our anger the most. This is why having peer supporters to lean on, individuals who have walked in similar situations, is crucial. The officer who has to make that decision to shoot or not shoot with terrible consequences. The firefighter who cannot enter into a building to save a child or the paramedic who has to decide through triage who gets the first ambulance ride to the hospital and who has to lay on the roadside until the next ambulance arrives. They need to speak to others who have walked that path before them to find out how they managed to survive the guilt, the shame, and the anger that surrounds such decisions. As professionals doing our jobs it's hard to admit to those feelings. But denial of our reactions and feelings is what keeps us injured and not able to move ahead.

Peer support is the foundation through which lived experience connects with empathy for those who have been traumatized. Peer support gets the medical or psychological help needed for an individual who reaches out. Peers support an individual through the healing process and offer reassurance and guidance. No single mental health service on its own can provide everything that is needed. All services and support need to work as one for the benefit of the sufferer.

Over time, with the help of family, friends, doctors, and peers, I started the journey toward positive growth. I learned to manage situations where I sometimes fall back with medication, therapy, and peer support. I now have an understanding of the importance of being self-aware and having a daily self-care plan.

# Echoes of the Mind
## Tim Grutzius

MY TRIGGER FOR PTSD BEGAN on a cold and lonely night in February of 1998 when our department responded to a car explosion. When the smoke cleared, I was informed that the victim was a colleague of mine who died by suicide. For the next sixteen years, I experienced the mood swings, anxiety, and the hypervigilance of undiagnosed PTSD.

In early 2014, I became a member of the Illinois Firefighter Peer Support Team. On the second day of training, I learned about firefighters and PTSD. It was then I realized that I had unresolved issues that needed attention. I sought the services of a licensed clinical professional counselor not only once, but twice in these last five years. The first round focused on the thoughts, the second time, emotions.

I am also a firm believer in holistic protocols that are rooted in the balance of mind, body, and spirit. In addition to the counseling, I still receive acupuncture treatments, massage therapy, chiropractic care, energy work (I am a reiki master), regular exercise (I am a personal trainer), and nutritional therapy. On May 28th, 2019 I retired from the Alsip Fire Department after twenty-five years of service. During that tenure, I learned two very important lessons.

The first lesson was garnered through my association with peer support: "Everyone brings a history with them into their chosen career." Some may come from abusive or alcoholic families and others may have been bullied. The prevailing stigma around mental health may prevent these individuals from sharing their stories with new colleagues. They suffer in silence and then the occupational exposures of being a first responder compounds this existing stress.

There will always be multiple generations working at the same time within our world and not everyone is going to be friends with the entire department. However, in the time we are with our colleagues (new and old alike), we should make every effort to learn as much as we can about them on an everyday basis. Deep sharing may not readily occur, but we will get a chance to see how they operate under their "norm." This will allow us to have a more heightened awareness when there is a deviation from said norm. Those of us who have walked this green mile can then feel more comfortable with having an honest conversation that opens with, "sit down my friend and tell me a story." Trust can or will be gained through strong mentorship.

Whether or not we believe it, first responder professions will profoundly change us from a psycho-emotional aspect. Some may have a higher resiliency factor than others yet can still be shaken to their core via occupational exposure. There are many other stakeholders besides the first responder themselves: spouses, significant others, family members—in other words, those who lift us up, our support system.

It is our duty to educate our support system on what it is like to be us. We do not have to share every gory detail—just the nuts and bolts. This can be accomplished one-on-one, or through spousal support outreach. My wife, Judy, is my best friend and I would have not made it to retirement without her undying love and support through the best and worst of times. On my last day, I presented Judy with her own "Retired Firefighter Wife" badge that was an honor she so richly deserved. Never leave behind those who lift us up. Do it every day, not just at the conclusion of your career. It's all about helping the next one in line.

In retirement, I am going to continue my peer support work, teach for the Firefighter Cancer Support Network as well as fitness education, volunteer for The Holistic Riding Equestrian Team, and obtain my life coach certification. For the past twenty-five years, I have worked on the reactive side of life. My future mission will be rooted in mentoring others on how to improve their quality of life from a preventative or restorative perspective. I want to do my part in making this world a better place to live.

*As an epilogue to my story, I want to let you know that I received closure from my friend's suicide in a most unexpected way. In February of 2019, I made my peer support educational outreach presentation to a local fire academy. My friend's daughter (who was five at the time of his death) was in that very academy class. She welcomed me with open arms and was completely fine with me talking about her dad (his name was not mentioned) to the rest of her class. Two weeks before my retirement, I attended her academy graduation. I exhaled and can truly say I walked away from this time-honored profession with a clean slate.*

The echoes of the mind will never let you forget, but in the face of adversity, always have the courage to take the high road. Mine started the first day I entered a therapist's office—and I never looked back.

# Through Darkness Beauty Grows
## Tracy Eldridge

A LOTUS FLOWER MUST grow through the dark and murky waters to reach the surface, to feel the sunshine, to be beautiful to many, and bring on an unexpected smile. I am a lotus flower.

Physical, mental, and emotional abuse consumed a large portion of my life. Most memories of that trauma lived on the surface and looped in my mind like a bad song. Over time fear, panic, and anxiety became my norm and ultimately became debilitating. In 2014, I was officially diagnosed with PTSD. My life was enveloped by trauma. In addition to my career in public safety hearing and seeing someone's worst day, from a young age I endured various types of abuse. As a young adult, I started a long history of abusive relationships, one of which resulted in a short-lived marriage. While we were only married for one year, the better part of our eight-year relationship was filled with aggressive and controlling behavior that would at times result in physical assault. Shortly after we were married in 1997, I started my life in public safety. I took a job as a 9-1-1 telecommunicator and then shortly after joined the local fire department as a call firefighter/EMT and ultimately obtained my paramedic license. I very quickly divorced the man who thought stealing from, cheating on, verbally, mentally, emotionally, and physically abusing a woman was what all the cool kids were doing. He was wrong! Over the next year, I worked hard to find my true self. I was not sure who I really was. I never recalled a time of normalcy, nor recalled a place where I felt inner peace.

As I was putting the shattered pieces of my life back together, I found my dream job and an amazing man who would love me enough to marry me and ultimately give me a beautiful home, two amazing daughters, a loving dog, and a life that many people dream of. For him, it was not easy. At times it is still not, however, he knows that who I am under the trauma is pretty awesome and worth the wait. I had built walls and he was the only one strong enough to break them down and sit with me in the darkness. When the time came, I took his hand and trusted his love and his intentions. For the first time in a long time, I felt a sense of safety and walked with him out of the darkness.

Fast forward to 2013, I had been the chief dispatcher for the 9-1-1 center that I had been working at for, at that time for seventeen years. I had a disagreement with my boss, who up until that day was my biggest fan. He turned on me and for the next three years, I endured aggressive, controlling, and harassing behavior from him and then ultimately the board of selectmen that I answered to. The Band-Aid was ripped off, the wound was now revealed. I never would have imagined I would have such a difficult fall from grace.

For years I taught 9-1-1 dispatchers nationwide how to take better care of themselves and educated them on PTSD. The irony was class after class, year after year, and little by little, I was sliding into a dark place, a place that continued to get darker over time. Before I knew it, it was so dark I could not find my way back to the light on my own. As I continued to teach these important lessons, I had blinders on and you could say, I was the carpenter living in an unfinished house or a plumber with a leaky faucet.

While there were many times I had hoped I would be plucked from Earth and delivered to Heaven, I knew deep down that suicide was not the way to stop the pain. I had, however, made peace with something happening to me accidentally. Then without warning, there was one day the demons almost got the better of me. I may never know what happened in that moment that pulled me out of that mindset that day, but I will forever give thanks to my God. I am truly blessed with my mess and now know why my story was written the way it was and how important it is to stop trying to steal the pen!

## Through Darkness, Beauty Grows

It will never be forgotten; it forever changed her life.

Evil reared its ugly head and covered her in strife.

She was a girl who lived a life giving everything her all.

No way was she at all prepared to take this sudden fall.

From the top of the world to the depths of hell; darkness filled her soul.

With each and every passing day her disease would take its toll.

On top of the world was where she sat, Lord knows she had it all.

The pain was so unbearable, her emotions were not her own.

Many times, she'd lie in bed and suffer in silence alone.

Until you have an invisible disease, one no one can see,

There's no way for you to know what life was like for me!

The fight never easy; good friends lost along the way,

But for those that stood beside her, in her heart they'll stay.

For years it had defined me, this disease and all its mess,

It took some time to realize, It was really just a test.

I passed this very important lesson and then the reason became quite clear;

I had to see the darkness so the sunlight could appear.

Through it all I learned some things that no one really knows;

There has to be some DARKNESS for that's where BEAUTY GROWS!

# i
## The Nothing that Never Happened
### William Young

TRUST ME, I WISH THAT my story had some catastrophic catalyst, some obvious origin that I could point to and say, "yeah, that's the moment that changed me forever." I guess if that was the case, I would've been able to sit down with some psychotherapist in a sweater vest and identify the incendiary incident that broke me.

But that's not how this thing works, not always; at least not for me. The manifestation of my malady, my malfunction, was a mystery. I have no harrowing tale of trauma and triumph. I have never had a sharpened toothbrush buried in the nape of my neck. I haven't torn a rotator cuff while wrestling with an inmate on the top tier, and I've never been held hostage by the homicidal henchmen of some big-time shot caller because I discovered their cache of crystal meth.

Nope, for me, it was the nothing that never happened.

For me, it was the stale smell of too many people being stuffed into a housing unit. It was the sound of the electric lock sliding into the reinforced frame. For me, it was navigating the constant current of negativity. For me, it was the walls and the wire; it was the beige and the gray and the vicious and vile things that the inmates say.

And I couldn't communicate my concerns to my counterparts, to my coworkers; no, they would call me weak or crazy. They would make comments and question my ability to be a correctional officer. They would suggest that I seek employment elsewhere. They would snicker as they shared their reasons that this job doesn't bother them.

I had heard it before. I had been in an office full of officers as they berated their brother, as they converged on their comrade like a committee of vultures chowing down on the rotting corpse of a caribou. Hell, I had even participated in the past.

There was no way that I was going to subject myself to that level of scrutiny, so I internalized my insecurities. I sucked it up. I put on my big boy pants. I portrayed myself as this big tough alpha-male that was unaffected by anything he saw or said or did.

Yep, inside the walls I had it all figured out, but at home, I was a mess. At home, I was a monster. I was angry and irritated and irrational. I would overreact when my son would forget to take out the trash and I would underreact when I learned about a relative suffering a heart attack. I was distant and disoriented and I was damaging relationships.

So, there I was, sitting and sulking and searching the internet for information. I needed to figure this thing out. I needed to get it together. I needed to be me again.

So, I started reading about burnout and fatigue and depression and suicide and I discovered that I was not alone, that my symptoms were not unique, and that there are definite negative side effects that an officer can suffer from working inside of a correctional facility. This revelation, this realization, was refreshing. I researched further to gain a better understanding of what was happening to me and I saw that what was happening to me was happening to correctional officers all over the world.

The common misconception among correctional staff is that there has to be some super violent traumatic event for the job, for the environment, to change us. We assume that because nothing has happened to us, nothing has happened to us.

And while we ponder our prognosis, while we reject our reality, finite fractures find each other and form one gigantic fault line felling our fragile façade. We break under the weight of decades of dismissiveness and we are forced to come to terms with the truth that this job, this environment, has changed us.

I had to acknowledge that I was wounded, that I was injured, and I needed help. And once I did, once I understood what was happening, I was able to fight it. But first, I had to submit to the fact that my symptoms and my current state of instability weren't the results of a singular situation, but rather, my condition was the culmination of everything that I had been throughout my career in corrections.

I began to feed myself with information; with tools, tips, and training to help me take back my life. I committed myself to combatting this contagion. I started to reengage in the outside world. I pushed myself to participate in positive activities that I was previously too "tired" to participate in.

Suddenly, my sense of foreboding and failure was replaced with an insatiable appetite to assist my brothers and sisters that were walking wounded through the halls of their respective facilities, facelessly fighting fatigue, silently suffering, afraid to reach out.

Officer wellness has now become my calling, my crusade, and I intend to shatter the stigma that surrounds these brave sentinels who selflessly serve their communities with professionalism, dignity, and honor.

I am still an emotionally numb, hyper-cynical, judgmental pile of sarcasm. My boots and my badge and my behavior all show signs of the struggle. I am a work in progress. Not quite cured, but no longer cursed.

# The Guy with All the Cool Stories

## Carl Waggett

THE WORLD IS FULL OF MYSTERIOUS PEOPLE. And who hasn't wanted to be the most interesting man in the room at one point or another? I know I have. You know the guy I'm talking about. He's mysterious and guarded, yet casual and nonchalant. He's friendly and approachable, yet cautious and calculated. And you can tell just by looking at his face that he has experienced the coolest shit ever. He's the kind of guy who everyone stands around at parties hanging on his every word and is the center of attention in a room full of people. He has the best analogies, the best expressions, and the best jokes. And he has the best stories ever—each one earned through some exciting adventure. Kurt Russell in *Backdraft* comes to mind. I wanted to be that guy. I wanted to be the guy with all the cool stories...until I had them.

As a young boy who loved watching movies growing up, I created an image of this broken-down man, misunderstood by everyone around him. Picture some combination of a secret spy, CIA agent, war hero, firefighter, and member of Delta Force. These are some of the strongest individuals in the world. However, movie culture had once again provided me with an over-the-top, exaggerated, and most importantly incorrect picture of these broken-down heroes. And in return, this image has helped create the stigma in our culture today—that tough guys don't ask for help and don't need it. But it has been my observation and experience that the individuals with the best stories are the ones that need help the most.

Because I wanted to be the guy with all the cool stories, I ran head-first into every situation. I wanted to see and experience it all. I wanted to gather all the material I could, knowing full well it would make for epic stories! Some of the older guys would try to warn me but I didn't listen. And as I got older (and hopefully wiser) I realized very quickly there was a cost to collecting these stories. And these stories began to compound one after another, over and over; piling up and weighing me down.

I remember the day that it hit me—when I realized that I was going to have to live this life. I wasn't going to die a heroic death at a young age, to forever be remembered for my bravery. Nope.

While living life, along the way I managed to gather friends and start a family and surround myself with people I love. And I didn't want to leave these people. And then I finally asked myself, "Who are all these stories for anyway?" I certainly didn't want to share them with my kids or my family. And I didn't want them anymore. So, what now?

Once you have these stories, they are yours for life. What I first considered a privilege was now a burden. So, what do you do with all of them? Where do all these stories go? You can't un-see things, and you can't erase a memory. This is why it is imperative to know how to manage your memories, stories, and experiences. And if you find you are struggling with this, seek help.

It's always the same at parties. I hate when someone finds out I'm a firefighter and asks, "What's the worst call you've ever been to? What's the grossest thing you've ever seen? Tell me all about it!" No thank you. I'd rather not. You really don't want to know.

There is nothing wrong with being the guy who has all the stories and sounds like he's lived ten lifetimes. The problem comes when the weight of those stories from your past starts breaking up the future you are so looking forward to. Stories are cool; I love to tell them. I love even more to hear a good one. But understand the stories you have are a powerful thing. If not handled correctly they will steal your livelihood right out from under you.

You (or your loved one) have made it through some crazy shit. That is why you are here reading this story. That means you have something special. The world needs to know the tales you have lived through. They need to hear them; perhaps not to the degree in which you have experienced them, but enough so that your stories can help. This way you can get back to being the single most interesting person in the room.

I don't want the stories anymore. So be careful what you wish for because you just might get it.

# The Value of Kindness

## Brad McKay

I WAS ONLY TWENTY-TWO WHEN I started my employment with York Regional Police in 1981. On October 28, 2014, I walked down those headquarters stairs for the last time as a police officer where my family was waiting for me and I was whisked off to celebrate my thirty-three-year career. In those days we were not psychologically prepared for what we would encounter—the scenes and the experiences that would sear themselves into your mind.

There was one particular call in 1984 that left me with many life lessons. I had no idea back then about the phenomenon of suicide by cop. But a young man named David was struggling with mental illness when he decided to come into Markham one night in September. The year before this he had been pulled from the Bloor street viaduct by Toronto Police before he could jump. On this night David decided to tell a restaurant owner that he was an off-duty police officer and he needed back up. Many of us responded promptly thinking it was a Toronto officer needing help. When one of my colleagues arrived, he was surprised by a man pointing a handgun at him. An exchange took place and David then ran into a crowded and noisy bar. When I arrived with another officer, we were met by shaken bouncers. We caught up with him inside the bar and paralleled together across the busy floor as he held the gun in combat stance while scanning and pointing at many people including me and my colleague. Communications were not working. As soon as I could get an unobstructed view, I shot him. He dropped immediately and so did the gun. He tried to get up, so we had to restrain him. Then he started to fade. The bullet had severed his aorta and he was later pronounced dead in hospital.

During the scuffle, I glanced over at the gun to make sure it was away from the man and I started planning how to secure it for safety. What I saw changed everything. The handle was broken open revealing a gas cartridge. It was not a real gun but an air pistol. He was not armed with a firearm.

The intensity of the emotions was overwhelming at that point. I knew I had done the right thing based on my training and what I saw. I could not have known it wasn't a real gun. I was congratulated for doing my job. But one of the things I now teach about is moral injury. The injury to your heart. Taking action where the results go against your moral compass. I didn't sign up to shoot unarmed people. So, despite the accolades, I was hurt. The incident rocked me to my soul.

There was no peer support system where I worked. But there were a number of people who walked with me through my exposure to trauma. Informal peer support systems exist in every community. Sometimes we don't realize how effective they are. Colleagues, friends, and my family were all there for me. How we treat and take care of our people matters.

The man that I shot had a family that cared for him. They had been trying to support David through his mental health struggles. He was the same age as me, twenty-five at the time. His mother wanted to make sure that the investigating detectives delivered a message to me. That message turned out to be the greatest gift I had ever received in my career. She wanted me to know that she knew I was just doing my job. She had forgiven me. I'm not sure how or where a mother who has just lost a child gets the energy and finds the kindness to do that. As a twenty-five-year-old officer with less than three years on the job, I wasn't sure what to do with that gift. I wasn't mature enough to completely understand it, but I knew it was significant.

There is a man that I follow over in the United Kingdom. His name is John Sutherland and he is a retired commander with the Metropolitan Police in London. He is releasing a second publication in 2020 and he has a meaningful TED talk. His message resonates with me and many that I connect with. His message is not complex. Simply, every contact leaves a trace, and how you treat people matters. I can assure you that the contact that was made from that grieving mother to me made a difference that cannot be described in words.

My path led me down the road of peer support. I have found through experience that our own trusted peers and colleagues can fill a great void between a suffering member and the path to resources. I was able to help form a Regional CISM Team and enhance peer and wellness systems in my service. In retirement,

I joined with Syd Gravel and started teaching and advising on the topic of peer support. I have joined some formal and informal groups and have been providing community support.

We don't always realize the power of an act of kindness. That one seemingly small act may make a difference in someone's life. It may be the one thing that matters most of all at that particular time.

His name was David Ross Jackson. And his mother may not have been able to save her son, but she did save me.

There are many lessons we can learn throughout a long career. The value of kindness was a powerful one for me. Those who are positive and kind will have many doors opened for them. It creates a good energy where people want to be.

So be kind to yourselves and to your inner circle of friends and family and take care of your peers. We are all worth it!

# What's the Worst that Could Happen?

## Angela Ponting

I WAS PHYSICALLY AND MENTALLY exhausted from being a single parent and sole financial provider, working in a field that required me to give one thousand percent of myself every day and put all of the emotions I was feeling in any particular moment on the back burner. I was physically and mentally exhausted from living with PTSD.

I was afraid that I was failing as a parent, medical practitioner, daughter, and as a friend. Fear led me to live a very calculated lifestyle. If my routine was disturbed or if something was out of place, it threw me into chaos. I was afraid of something coming into my life and disrupting the order I had built around myself as a coping mechanism for simply existing. I went through life mechanically. Each day a repeat of the day before, nothing out of routine, nothing out of order. There was fun, but the fun was planned as much as the meals we ate were planned. Directions were researched well in advance, snacks and drinks were packed and itineraries made. God forbid someone strayed from the itinerary. If there was any change in plan, I would panic and become upset and angry. Fun was always structured and had a time limit. I couldn't ever give up control and be spontaneous.

Lack of control leads to fear. That fear almost made me take my own life. It was at the moment when I was faced with a choice of whether to live or die that I realized *if* I was going to choose life, I was going to really live and not simply exist and go through life mechanically. *If* I chose life, I was going to have to face my fears and make some serious changes. I chose life.

That choice was a rebirth. I had to relearn simple tasks like walking my dog, driving my car, and going shopping for food. These may not seem monumental, but for someone who lives with PSTD, they are huge. My life was still very structured. Get up, make my bed, walk the dog, but instead of these being tasks, they were all accomplishments. I took pride in making my bed, in completing a lap around the neighborhood with the dog, and even in making a grilled cheese sandwich!

Grilled cheese sandwiches turned into roasted chicken dinners; walks around the neighborhood became walks on the beach. I began to take pride in the milestones I reached. Drive throughs soon became dine-in restaurants, which then became outdoor patios. I realized I was starting to interact with people again, even if it meant just smiling at a stranger. I was able to go to small arenas to watch my son play hockey again. Standing with my back near a wall turned into sitting on the inside of the arena; sitting inside turned into sitting with other people so that I could cheer my child on. Small arenas turned into OHL arenas. I was thinking that one day I would be able to go to a festival or a concert again. I started to feel a sense of hope.

How with all of these planned outings was I actually living again and giving up control? There were times when things didn't go as planned. For instance, my go-to parking spot on a certain street was not accessible one hockey game and I was in sheer terror. What now? My son in all of his wisdom said, "How about we just turn down the next street and see what we find?"

What? See what we find? What was the worst that could happen? We turned down the next street and parked in a different spot. Nothing bad happened.

Recently, my son asked me to take him and a friend to a large amusement park. It would require driving two hours to and from the park and spending a day in the hot, blazing sun. What is the worst that could happen? I mapped the route, packed snacks, an umbrella, a book, and a lawn chair because I had planned to drop the boys off and sit outside under a tree, reading, drinking water, and consuming my snacks. The boys were talking about the rides they wanted to go on and I was thinking about how it must be fun to be young and not have a care or fear in the world. When was the last time I threw caution to the wind, strayed from a plan, and just let myself have a good time? The boys convinced me to come into the park with them. What is the worst that could happen?

We got our tickets and they immediately took me to the "kiddie land" and said that we could start on those rides, but that they really wanted me to come on the adult rides with them. We started with a baby roller coaster and graduated from there. I caught myself laughing and smiling and feeling excited and nervous about where they would lead me to next. Ride after ride, with the boys supportively coaxing me on, and being patient, we made our way around the park. In fact, I went on three record-setting roller coasters!

Were my eyes shut the entire time? Yes, but the point is, I didn't die, nothing bad happened, and I laughed for an entire day. This was living! This was being free. This was giving up all control to some teenage kids, a waist restraint on a ride, and a seventy-five-meter drop. This was me finding out the worst that could happen was more likely fiction in my head than actual reality. This was me looking fear in the face and telling it to back up because I was going to walk straight by.

# I'm Just a Volunteer

## Andrew Moritz

I'M JUST A VOLUNTEER. That's what I have always called myself. I don't get paid for what I do. I grew up around it. There was never a question in my mind about what I would do. My goal has always been to help my neighbors in, what for many, is the worst time of their lives. I never imagined the influence it would have on me. Yet it molded who I have become and for that I am truly blessed.

I am a volunteer firefighter as was my grandpa and uncle—three generations. My grandpa joined in the 1970s when he moved our family from the city to a small town; the same blue-collar city where I now raise my daughter with my wife. A city best known for its shared portion of a mighty waterfall and international border with Canada.

I grew up around the fire hall. I grew to love the old guys, playing euchre after setting up the hall for bingo the next evening. I can still see them sitting at the table in the member's room.

Smoking cherry pipe tobacco, drinking black coffee, talking about the calls or goings-on in our little corner of the world. Some were farmers, other factory workers.

I can still see much of what I have done over the last eighteen years of my volunteer and paid career in EMS (emergency medical services). The sounds, smells, sights—in certain moments I can recall the textures of my gear as I responded to these moments. It may be hard to believe but I can recall so much. Sometimes at will, other times almost at random. The memories come on like waves, almost as powerful as those on Lake Erie that come crashing ashore amidst a winter storm.

I stepped away from the service for about three years to raise my daughter and marry the most amazing woman I have ever met. A time I should have been on top of the world. It was in the quiet moments, or moments where I wasn't sure if I was making the best decision, that these waves would come crashing ashore. I would wake in the middle of the night, feeling as though I ran a marathon; my heart beating from my chest, unable to re-center myself. Sometimes it was a nightmare about a call I had taken. Other times it was outlandish fears that something left on may have started a fire, much like the first house I responded to. The family had left on vacation and a half-hour later nearly their entire home was ablaze, all from the top of a piece of Tupperware jamming against the heating element in the dishwasher.

So many nights I would wander our little two-bedroom apartment looking for things or reasons why I couldn't sleep. Even worse was sitting at family dinner and though I was looking into my wife's eyes I was seeing the face of a young girl after a diabetic episode. A girl that was with an older man who turned out not to be her uncle, but a man with illicit intentions who had brought girls of similar age to this hotel many times before. What led to this discovery was her passing out from low blood sugar. She was only willing to confide in me, a twenty-year-old kid at the time.

After so many of these moments where my wife would look at me but see that I was not there, she finally asked what was going on. Me not being present nearly broke us. How could I ever put into words that I was still in a basement watching the fire licking the boards above me and my partner's heads?

It all felt too much—like opening Pandora's Box. A mere peek and the demons I had for so long wrestled to hold down would go running every which way, never to be reeled back in again. At that point, I confessed to her what had been going on. Through teary eyes, she said just two words that started me on my path of recovery. "It's okay." The only acceptance I needed. We spent days searching, calling, and discussing what we should do until we found a doctor who handled post-traumatic stress disorder (PTSD).

After a handful of meetings, he looked at me and confirmed I did indeed have PTSD caused by the many experiences I encountered in my career to date. While grateful there was a diagnosis, it made the next steps slightly harder because we could not pinpoint one specific call or occurrence. However, we did establish a working treatment which I still use today. So while I may see myself to be just a volunteer, PTSD doesn't care. PTSD doesn't care if I'm a paid firefighter or a volunteer. It does not care if I'm an active member or long retired. The way I see it if PTSD doesn't care, then neither do I. To most, PTSD is a difficult and negative thing. But for me, I see it as a gift—something that I happily carry as part of my past and in my continuous service to my community.

# Our Darkest Nights are Our Truest Gifts
## Terrance Kosikar

I DIDN'T CARE IF I SHIT MYSELF, all I could think was, "fuck," this is how they are going to find me, face down in puke, lips dried up, forty pounds underweight, foaming at the mouth, table full of meth and crack cocaine, ashes and cigarette butts everywhere, some prostitute's panties and socks still laying on the bed, while porn plays on the television beside me.

I laid on the floor as the bugs crawled over my dead body, down my arms, between my toes, like millions of tiny little ants eating me alive from the inside out—the most torturous way to die.

I could hear the doctors and nurses rushing to bring me back to life. I could hear the sirens, the voices, endless visions of people screaming, laughing, and crying while thousands of thoughts and emotions flooded my every breath.

Where am I? Why am I?

The stenchful smell as I lay drenched in a deathly odor of sweat; my veins cold and shivering uncontrollably.

I could feel my skin tight to my bones, visions and sounds of what seemed to be every single person in my entire life who had talked or stabbed me in the back, were all doing so at the same time right here at my death sentence, they laugh, your weak, they giggle, the guilt, the shame, the hurt, the pain, unbearable nor describable in human language.

I risked my life for you, my health for you, my family for you. I breathed for you, I jumped up at three in the morning and rushed to the firehall knowing you needed me, my service, my strength, my training, my protection, our care.

I did not owe it. I did not have to—this is just who we are.

In that moment, I felt like I had nothing left—I'd been stripped of my family, my friends, my career, hopes and dreams, my pride, and my sanity.

It's not that I wanted to die—I felt like I was already dead.

How does one explain what goes on in the mind from a lifetime of dancing in the deepest, darkest depths of the devil's belly? The utter insanity that riddles one's every breath, spiritually disconnected from self, questioning our very existence, not asking "why should I live" but rather "how can I live?"

I woke from my daze; homeless, hopeless, hungry, and in search of which way to turn to get out of this mental maze.

I soon found myself hundreds of kilometers away from humans, deep in the backcountry mountains of British Columbia in Canada. I was shivering cold, dope sick, my withdrawals unbearable, and questioning my sanity. I needed to get warm, eat, and survive.

Winter was coming. Cold rain trickled down my face as I stood on the side of the mountain felling a tree in the First Nations St'at'imc territory when a native man Ambie appeared in a camouflage jacket with the eyes of a lion with his firearm beside him. Would this be my demise?

I humbly explained my situation and instead of burying me alive he shared his land, his trees, his fish, and half of a freshly killed deer with me, a total stranger. This was genuine compassion from a man who still lived by "the old ways."

The gift of hope was given with the seed he planted. It is now up to me to water this seed and begin to understand my purpose on this Earth by planting many more around the world.

We can learn much about ourselves while in the process of digging ourselves out from the grave. Many tears will be shed, hard work indeed, but we can reconnect the spirit to self and find self-love, our passion, our goals and dreams, and community with no room for greed. We must live selflessly in order to succeed. In my opinion, the only thing wrong with PTSD is the name. It is by far the most disrespectful, dishonorable label we can ever put on any human.

How a natural response to danger can ever be viewed as a medically diagnosed disorder is beyond me.

With awareness comes education, with education comes knowledge, with knowledge we are better able to help others have a better understanding of post-traumatic stress, and what it is, how it's caused and most importantly, how to manage and prevent the "unprocessed, bound energy" from ruining our lives.

Since attempting suicide in 2015, we now run a nonprofit Camp My Way Wilderness program for first responders, veterans, at-risk youth, and their families who have been affected by post-traumatic stress.

We have helped change provincial legislation and amended the Workers Compensation Act of British Columbia—"Presumption of Illness," that now gives first responders who have been diagnosed with PTSD immediate help without the hoops, along with earning an honorary degree in Philosophy from the College of Certified Psych physiologists.

We have flipped 400-pound tractor tires for weeks on end up glaciers and across mountains while shackled in 70 pounds of solid steel chains thousands of miles across the country and around the world to raise awareness and help destigmatize PTSD. We now travel to many countries to help educate emergency service professionals, government officials, high school and university students to bring more knowledge and a better understanding of post-traumatic stress.

Truth, love, and rest are our most powerful weapon.

# i'
## Your i'Mpossible Story
### (You)

# Author Biographies

**Jean-Guy Poirier** was born and raised in a small city in Eastern Ontario, Canada. He moved to Southeastern Ontario in his early twenties and joined the local volunteer fire department in 2005. During his eleven years in the department, he faced numerous traumatic events which ultimately led him to being diagnosed with posttraumatic stress disorder in May 2017. He then decided to form a Facebook page that would focus on PTSD. In October 2018, Poirier developed the first PTSD support group in his area. The program will be operating in four different communities beginning in Fall 2019.

**Lee J. Plummer** is a disabled veteran aspiring to become an author as he writes the truth to his life's story. He deployed to Afghanistan in 2010 during Operation Enduring Freedom on convoy security element/line haul as a Navy Seabee in the reserves—after which he struggled for many years and still does as he fights for his disability benefits. In 2018, he completed his associates in general studies and is now reaching for his dreams as an artist/writer. You can find his writing at https://leejplummer.wixsite.com/ambitiouslycreative

or at Twitter.com/leejplummer advocating for mental health through fitness and much more.

An addictions counsellor by trade, **John Arenburg** spent fifteen years in the volunteer fire service and nearly twenty years working in long-term care, helping those with mental disabilities and mental illness. Off work because of his mental health injury, PTSD, John dedicates his time to his blog, The Road to Mental Wellness, telling his story about his struggles with PTSD, depression, and anxiety, hoping it will resonate with others. He regularly meets with people, both online and in person to help them with their mental health struggles. He lives in Nova Scotia with his partner and two children. https://www.theroadtomentalwellness.com.

**Grant Bourne** is a retired U.S. Marine, philanthropist, lover of life, and professional goofball. If you don't find him spending time with his girlfriend and kiddo, you can probably find him on one of his motorcycles riding down the road or camping. From January 1st, 2018 to November 5th, 2018 Grant rode over 100,000 miles in the United States to raise awareness for suicide and suicide prevention. These days, no matter where he is or what he is doing, you will always hear him ask almost every person that he interacts with, "how are you doing?"

**Linda Green** worked thirty-two years with the California Department of Forestry and Fire Protection. In 2015 she was the Incident Commander the first night of the Valley Fire, where she suffered her post-traumatic stress injury. Linda volunteers at the West Coast Post-Traumatic Retreat and is now on the Board of

Trustees of the First Responder Support Network, the parent organization of WCPR. Linda is a Certified High-Performance Coach and is the author of *Solving the Post-Traumatic Brain Injury Puzzle: A First Responder's GPS.* She lives in California with her husband of thirty-one years, and their two rescue dogs.

**Marie-Julie Cosenzo** was born and raised in Ottawa, Canada, by wonderful parents. She has one younger brother, who's an incredible uncle to her son and daughter. She has been featured in educational videos for French and English language colleges throughout Canada, sharing her experiences as a former paramedic battling mental illness. She has a blog (mariejuliesptsd.wordpress.com), where she occasionally shares her struggles and successes. She can often be found knitting around a campfire, painting at home, or playing soccer. She hopes to form a therapy dog team with her beloved dog Elsa, calming nervous travelers at the Ottawa International Airport.

**Matt McGregor** is a former first responder from Canada. His life has been plagued by trauma and tragedy from a very early age, yet he continues to write about his experiences to help others in darkness. His survival is nothing short of a miracle due the extreme nature of things he has endured. He has come close to taking his life on numerous occasions and still fights to find his way through his own darkness but refuses to give up because he believes his purpose was to suffer in order to help others.

**Myles Hall** is a retired police officer. After having served twenty years in the Royal Canadian Mounted Police from 1993 to 2013, he was diagnosed with PTSD in 2018. Myles wrote a memoir of his time in policing as a collection of short stories entitled *The Adventures of Mylo the Mountie*, a chronicle of the "unbelievable" circumstances he found himself in and how those experiences effected his mental health.

**Paula Elias** (nee Dawes) has been a firefighter with Toronto Fire Services since 2002. She is the mother of two happy, adaptable kids and the wife of one easygoing and tolerant husband.

**Rob Leathen** is a twenty-seven-year veteran of the fire service holding the rank of Acting Platoon Chief for a mid-sized fire department in Ontario, Canada. He has held a variety of roles throughout his career including volunteer firefighter, fire dispatcher, career firefighter, acting captain, captain, and acting platoon chief. Rob has also been involved in his local firefighter association on the health and safety committee and association President on two separate occasions. Rob is a vocal advocate for first responder mental health using his lived experience with PTSD and depression to help educate others through talks, presentations, and writing.

**Sarah Roselli** is a twenty-one-year-old student studying occupational therapy at Jefferson University. Sarah has been working as an EMT since 2018 and volunteers with her town's emergency rescue squad.

**Sylvio (Syd) A Gravel,** M.O.M., Staff Sergeant (retired), Ottawa Police Service, Canada, is a thirty-one-year veteran, diagnosed with PTSD in 1987 who retired in 2009. He is the cofounder of a post shooting trauma peer support team established in 1988 and still in existence today. He is the author of two books, *56 Seconds* and *How to Survive PTSD and Build Peer Support* and co-author of *Walk the Talk*. Today, he teaches peer support at the national and international level and still keeps himself grounded by volunteering with Badge of Life Canada and his post shooting trauma group.

After a twenty-five-year career with the Alsip Fire Department, **Tim Grutzius** retired at the rank of Lieutenant in 2019. He volunteers for Illinois Firefighter Peer Support, Firefighter Cancer Support Network, and the Holistic Riding Equestrian Team. Additionally, Tim is a personal trainer, reiki master, and life coach candidate. He has a startup wellness business (Cent'Anni Life) with a mission of making this world a better place to live for all. For twenty-three years Tim has been married to his best friend and wife Judy who has his undying gratitude for her years of support as a firefighter's wife.

**Tracy Eldridge** is the Public Safety Community Engagement Manager at RapidSOS, she has played a significant role in delivering new life-saving technology to public safety. She began her public safety career in 1997 as a 9-1-1 dispatcher and then became a Chief Dispatcher 2003. She serves as a firefighter/EMT on her local fire department. As an instructor for the Public Safety Group she enjoys traveling nationwide teaching telecommunicators, EMTs and firefighters. Tracy has also been recognized nationally for her efforts to bring awareness to PTSD and the 9-1-1 telecommunicator.

**William Young** is a seasoned correctional officer and mental health advocate. Because of his extensive exposure to trauma and the aftermath, William is determined to assist his fellow brothers and sisters by helping them identify, manage, and reverse the side effects and symptoms that surface when subjected to situations that are considered just "part of the job." His book, *When Home Becomes a Housing Unit* addresses the issues that arise when an officer's work follows them home. William would like to hear from you. You can contact him at Justcorrections@gmail.com or visit his Facebook page at www.facebook.com/wllmyoung.

**Carl Waggett** is a firefighter, blogger, and speaker at PTSD Bunker Gear for Your Brain.

**Brad McKay** retired after thirty-three years of service with York Regional Police in Canada. He directs his own company 228 Solutions. Brad co-created the York Region CISM Team in 1996 and holds an advisor position. Brad started the OSI Prevention and Response Unit for YRP. As a certified trauma services specialist, Brad has responded to and coordinated over a thousand interventions for front line responders and their families. He teaches peer support in North America and the United Kingdom. He co-authored *Walk the Talk* a peer support systems guide.

**Angela Ponting** is a single mother of one boy. She has worked as a Nurse for eight years. Angela is a mental health and suicide prevention advocate. She is a regional director of Wings of Change as well as a chapter facilitator. Angela is currently pursuing a certificate in Mental Health and Psychiatric Nursing. By sharing her own story, she hopes to help reduce the stigma associated with living with a mental illness not only in her profession but in society as a whole.

**Andrew Moritz** is a third-generation volunteer firefighter, active for nearly eighteen years total. He is married to an amazing woman Haley and together they have a beautiful five-year-old daughter Jamie. When not working, he is still active in the fire service. Their family enjoys traveling and is planning a Disney cruise. He is an avid gamer who enjoys posting to YouTube, and also enjoys fishing and repairing his grandfather's Lionel trains. Andrew would like to someday write more about his experiences and help fellow first responders share their stories. He is an active advocate for PTSD awareness and treatment.

**Terrance Kosikar** was a first responder to a fatal accident on opening day of the 2010 Winter Olympics in Vancouver. Although well trained in a myriad of life-saving techniques, he was not prepared to deal with the emotional impact. As a result of the fatality, Kosikar developed PTSD that launched him into a very costly downward spiral. During several years of severe depression, he abused substances and attempted suicide. Kosikar lost his family, career, and nearly his life. Pushed to the breaking point, Kosikar found salvation within. Escaping to the backcountry, he found peace and purpose in Mother Nature.

## ABOUT THE CURATORS

Joshua Rivedal is the creator and founder of Changing Minds: A Mental Health Based Curriculum and **The i'Mpossible Project**. He is trained in community counseling from the Southern California Counseling Center; human capital management with an emphasis in coaching from NYU; and is also trained in QPR, ASIST, and the teacher's edition of emotional intelligence at Yale University's Center for Emotional Intelligence. He has spoken about suicide prevention, mental health, diversity, anti-bullying, and storytelling across the U.S., Canada, the U.K., and Australia. He wrote and developed the one-man play, *Kicking My Blue Genes in The Butt* (KMBB), which has toured extensively throughout the world paired with suicide prevention education. His memoir *The Gospel According to Josh: A 28-Year Gentile Bar Mitzvah*, based on KMBB, is on The American Foundation for Suicide Prevention's recommended reading list. His second book, The i'Mpossible Project: Volume 1—*Reengaging with Life, Creating a New You*, debuted #1 in its category on Amazon in January 2016. There are currently four books in the i'Mpossible Project series. He is a co-author of three journal papers, one on the trajectory of the survivor of suicide loss, another on the art of living with chronic illness, the third on surviving trauma. www.iampossibleproject.com.

Kathleen Myre is a Certified Recovery Peer Specialist and a certified WRAP (Wellness Recovery Action Plan) facilitator in the state of Florida. She is a passionate advocate for mental health awareness and suicide prevention on a local and global scale. Kathleen currently works as a volunteer for Peer Support Space, a non-profit organization in Kissimmee, Florida, where she shares her lived experienced with depression and anxiety to give hope to others during their own recovery. Her primary goal is to eradicate the stigma surrounding mental illnesses so others will seek help in their own moment of need.

## ALSO BY JOSHUA RIVEDAL

*The Gospel According to Josh:*
*A 28-Year Gentile Bar Mitzvah*
(Based on the one-man show
*Kicking My Blue Genes in the Butt*)

By the time Joshua Rivedal turned twenty-five, he thought he'd have the perfect life—a few years singing on Broadway, followed by a starring role in his own television show. After which, his getaway home in the Hamptons would be featured in Better Homes & Gardens, and his face would grace the cover of the National Enquirer as Bigfoot's not-so-secret lover.

Instead, his resume is filled with an assortment of minor league theatre and an appearance on The Maury Povich Show—a career sidetracked by his father's suicide, a lawsuit from his mother over his inheritance, and a break-up with his long-term girlfriend.

Tortured by his thoughts, he finds himself on the ledge of a fourth-floor window, contemplating jumping out to inherit his familial legacy. In turn he must reach out to the only person who can help before it's too late.

Available on Amazon, Kindle, B&N.com. and at
www.iampossibleproject.com/the-gospel-according-to-josh

# The i'Mpossible Project: Volume I
*Reengaging with Life, Creating a New You*

Storytelling is one of our oldest traditions. Stories can make us laugh or cry... or both at the same time. They can teach, inspire and even ignite an entire movement.

*The i'Mpossible Project* is a collection of powerful stories. They're gritty, deep, heartwarming... and guaranteed to help you discover new possibilities in your life.

These stories are all about overcoming obstacles, reengaging with life, and creating new possibilities—a son's homicide, a transgender man finding love, coming back from the brink of suicide, finding your funny in the face of overwhelming odds, and more...

If you're ready to create new possibilities in your life, you need to read this book!

Available on Amazon, Kindle, B&N.com. and at
www.iampossibleproject.com/one

# The i'Mpossible Project: Volume II
*Changing Minds, Breaking Stigma,*
*Achieving the Impossible*

Storytelling is one of our oldest and greatest human achievements. Stories can enchant, empower, inspire, motivate, and even change the course of humankind. Volume 2 of the i'Mpossible Project-- Changing Minds, Breaking Stigma, Achieving the Impossible, offers another 50 life-changing stories.

These are true tales from real people who have achieved incredible feats in the face of overwhelming odds, showing that impossible is just a state of mind—and that anything is possible.

You'll read about: an entrepreneur using his battle with alcohol abuse to empower others; an award winning high school student who battled bullying, self-harm, and an eating disorder to become her best self; and an actor who calls his depression "my frenemy Dewayne."

If you're looking to turn "impossible" into "possible" in your world... you need to read this book!

Available on Amazon, Kindle, B&N.com. and at
www.iampossibleproject.com/two

# The i'Mpossible Project
## Lemonade Stand: Volume I & II

Overcoming trauma or a major obstacle in life takes courage—a word that originally meant, "to speak one's mind by telling all one's heart."

The ability to change a negative into a positive, to turn lemons into lemonade, and to then share that recipe with the world to prevent others from suffering—it's one of the most beautiful things a person can do.

These stories and storytellers in Lemonade Stand are full of heart and are the definition of courage. Inside you'll find a transforming look at a young woman who was assaulted by her best friend, a father navigating raising newborn triplets, and a man who lost his eyesight in a tragic accident and proved that you don't need eyes to truly see.

When life gives you lemons, squeeze, add sugar and pick up a copy of The i'Mpossible Project's Lemonade Stand: Volume I.

Available on Amazon, Kindle, B&N.com. and at
www.iampossibleproject.com/lemonade

## A Mental Health Based Curriculum

Changing Minds is programming and curriculum that combines lecture, storytelling, group discussion, and improv theatre to enhance emotional development—providing hope, help, and lifesaving skills. Changing Minds is available for grades K-12, college, CEUs, and professional development.

There are five (5), sixty (60) minute modules:

- The Basics of Mental Health
- Developing Coping Skills
- Storytelling and Support Systems (promoting Help-Seeking and Help-Offering behavior)
- Living with/Supporting a Person with a Mental Health Condition
- Helping Yourself or a Friend in Suicidal Crisis

Five more modules are being developed on: Diversity, Emotional Intelligence, Anti-Bullying, and Substance Abuse.

www.changingmindsstrong.com

www.ingramcontent.com/pod-product-compliance
Lightning Source LLC
Chambersburg PA
CBHW020301030426
42336CB00010B/850